foreword

There is something about eating meat off the bone that speaks to the inner carnivore in all of us. Whether they are beef or pork, back or side, ribs are a favourite of get-togethers and backyard barbecues throughout the nation.

Done right, ribs can be happiness on a plate. Done wrong, they can rival shoe leather in texture. When cooking ribs, remember that "low and slow" is the key to succulent, fall-off-the-bone meat. In other words, to keep them tender, ribs should be cooked slowly over low heat rather than quickly over high heat. On a gas barbecue, you'll get best results by cooking the ribs with the indirect method, over an unlit burner beside the lit burner. Also, remove the membrane or "silver skin" before cooking or marinating the ribs.

Whether you prefer your ribs sauced or rubbed, baked, roasted or barbecued, you'll find the recipes you need in this book. So roll up your sleeves and dig in...and expect to get a little messy.

Jean Paré

battered dry ribs

Salty and slightly sweet, these golden brown ribs are the perfect finger food. Delicious!

Sweet and sour cut pork ribs, cut into 1-bone portions	3 lbs.	1.4 kg
Hoisin sauce	3 tbsp.	45 mL
Apple cider vinegar	2 tbsp.	30 mL
Brown sugar, packed	2 tbsp.	30 mL
Water	2 tbsp.	30 mL
Garlic clove, minced (or 1/4 tsp., 1 mL, powder)	1	1
Salt	2 tsp.	10 mL
All-purpose flour	1/3 cup	75 mL
Large eggs	4	4

Cooking oil, for deep-frying

In large pot or Dutch oven, boil ribs in enough water to cover for 20 minutes. Drain. Cool. Blot dry.

Combine next 6 ingredients in large bowl. Stir.

Add flour. Mix. Add eggs, 1 at a time, stirring well with whisk after each addition, until batter is smooth. Add ribs. Stir until coated.

Deep-fry, in 2 or 3 batches, in hot (375°F, 190°C) cooking oil for about 2 minutes, stirring often, until browned. Remove to paper towels to drain. Makes about 100 ribs. Serves 16.

1 serving: 290 Calories; 21 g Total Fat (9 g Mono, 2.5 g Poly, 7 g Sat); 115 mg Cholesterol; 5 g Carbohydrate (0 g Fibre, 2 g Sugar); 18 g Protein; 430 mg Sodium

chinese sweet and sour ribs

This bright, colourful dish is delicious!

Reserved pineapple juice	1/4 cup	60 mL
Cornstarch	2 tsp.	10 mL
Ketchup	1/3 cup	75 mL
White vinegar	3 tbsp.	45 mL
Dry sherry	2 tbsp.	30 mL
Water	1 tbsp.	15 mL
Granulated sugar	2 tbsp.	30 mL
Soy sauce	2 tbsp.	30 mL
Egg yolk (large)	1	1
Sweet and sour cut pork ribs, cut into 1-bone portions	3 lbs.	1.4 kg
Cornstarch	1/2 cup	125 mL
Cooking oil, for deep-frying		
Cooking oil	1 tbsp.	15 mL
Medium onion, cut into thin wedges	1	1
Can of pineapple tidbits (14 oz., 398 mL), drained and juice reserved	1	1
Chopped red pepper	1 cup	250 mL

Stir pineapple juice into first amount of cornstarch in small bowl. Add next 4 ingredients. Stir. Set aside.

Combine sugar, soy sauce and egg yolk in medium bowl. Add pork. Toss until coated. Marinate in refrigerator for 1 hour.

Remove pork from marinade. Coat pork with second amount of cornstarch. Deep-fry in hot (350°F, 175°C) cooking oil for about 3 minutes until cooked and golden brown. Remove to paper towels to drain.

Heat wok or large frying pan on medium-high. Add second amount of cooking oil. Add onion. Stir-fry for about 3 minutes until onion is softened. Add pineapple, red pepper and pork. Stir sauce. Add to pork mixture. Stir-fry until pork is coated and heated through. Makes 8 cups (2 L).

1 cup (250 mL): 550 Calories; 39 g Total Fat (18 g Mono, 4.5 g Poly, 13 g Sat); 115 mg Cholesterol; 23 g Carbohydrate (1 g Fibre, 14 g Sugar); 34 g Protein; 490 mg Sodium

braised hoisin spareribs

Hoisin and five-spice powder lend an aromatic Asian influence to these small morsels with a lively chili heat. Serve with finger bowls so your guests can engage in a more refined eating experience.

Sweet and sour cut pork ribs (breastbone removed)	1 1/2 lbs.	680 g
Hoisin sauce	1/4 cup	60 mL
Sweet chili sauce	1/4 cup	60 mL
Sesame oil	2 tbsp.	30 mL
Soy sauce	2 tbsp.	30 mL
Water	2 tbsp.	30 mL
Garlic cloves, minced	2	2
Chinese five-spice powder	1 tsp.	5 mL

Place ribs, bone side down, in baking pan.

Stir remaining 7 ingredients until smooth. Pour 2/3 cup (150 mL) of sauce mixture over ribs. Bake, covered, in a 350°F (175°C) oven for 30 minutes. Bake, uncovered, for about 45 minutes, basting with pan juices and remaining sauce mixture, until fully cooked and tender. Cover with foil and let stand for 10 minutes. Transfer to cutting board and cut ribs into 1-bone portions. Makes about 12 ribs.

1 rib: 180 Calories; 13 g Total Fat (5 g Mono, 5 g Poly, 4.5 g Sat); 40 mg Cholesterol; 5 g Carbohydrate (0 g Fibre, 2 g Sugar); 11 g Protein; 320 mg Sodium

baked smoky sweet and sour ribs

Sweet, sour, spicy and tender. Need we say more?

Pork side ribs, cut into 2 or 3 rib potions	5 lbs.	2.3 kg
Brown sugar, packed	3/4 cup	175 mL
Chili powder	1/2 tsp.	2 mL
Apple cider vinegar	3/4 cup	175 mL
Ketchup	1/2 cup	125 mL
Small onion, chopped	1	1
Worcestershire sauce	2 tbsp.	30 mL
Water	1/2 cup	125 mL
Salt	1/2 tsp.	2 mL
Cornstarch	1 tbsp.	15 mL
Dry mustard	1 tsp.	5 mL
Liquid smoke	1/8 tsp.	0.5 mL

In large uncovered pot or Dutch oven, boil ribs for 15 minutes in enough water to cover. Drain. Arrange ribs in small roaster.

Mix remaining 11 ingredients in medium bowl. Pour over ribs. Bake, covered, in 350°F (175°C) oven for 1 to 1 1/2 hours until pork is falling-off-the-bone tender. Serves 6.

1 serving: 900 Calories; 64 g Total Fat (0 g Mono, 0 g Poly, 21 g Sat); 220 mg Cholesterol; 36 g Carbohydrate (0 g Fibre, 33 g Sugar); 42 g Protein; 750 mg Sodium

spicy tamarind ribs

Tamarind and lemon grass give these ribs an exotic flair, while the chili pepper adds a touch of heat. Back ribs also work wonderfully in this recipe.

Sweet and sour cut pork ribs, trimmed of fat, cut into 1-bone portions (see Tip, page 64)	3 lbs.	1.4 kg
Sliced lemon grass, bulbs only	1/2 cup	125 mL
Tamarind liquid	1/2 cup	125 mL
Brown sugar, packed	1/4 cup	60 mL
Liquid honey	1/4 cup	60 mL
Soy sauce	1/4 cup	60 mL
Garlic cloves, chopped	4	4
Small red chili peppers, chopped (see Tip, page 64)	5	5

Put ribs into large resealable freezer bag.

Process remaining 7 ingredients in blender or food processor until smooth. Pour over ribs and marinate in refrigerator for 2 hours. Arrange ribs in single layer in greased 9 x 13 inch (23 x 33 cm) baking dish and pour marinade over top. Cover with foil and cook in 350°F (175°C) oven for 1 hour until tender. Remove cover and skim any fat. Cook, uncovered, for an additional hour, stirring every 10 minutes, until glazed. Serves 4.

1 serving: 910 Calories; 55 g Total Fat (24 g Mono, 5 g Poly, 21 g Sat); 210 mg Cholesterol; 43 g Carbohydrate (1 g Fibre, 36 g Sugar); 60 g Protein; 1160 mg Sodium

redneck ribs

Tasty, tender ribs with southern smoked spices that will please the whole family. Pineapple juice helps tenderize the pork, and peanuts give it a unique crunch.

Pork rib sections, 10 to 13 ribs each	2	2
Pork stock or water	6 cups	1.5 L
Pineapple juice	2 cups	500 mL
Bay leaves	2	2
Peppercorns	10	10
Garlic cloves, halved	5	5
Brown sugar	1/4 cup	60 mL
Salt	1 tsp.	5 mL
Tomato paste	1/2 cup	125 mL
Honey	1/4 cup	60 mL
Agave syrup	2 tbsp.	30 mL
Ground cinnamon	1/4 tsp.	1 mL
Ground cloves	1/8 tsp.	0.5 mL
Smoked paprika	1/2 tsp.	2 mL
Hot pepper sauce	2 tsp.	10 mL
Prepared mustard	1 tbsp.	15 mL
Unsalted peanuts, chopped	1/4 cup	60 mL

Lay ribs flat in large roasting pan. Combine next 7 ingredients in medium bowl. Pour over ribs so that liquid almost fully covers ribs—add more water to pan if necessary. Roast in 350°F (175°C) oven until meat becomes loose on bone, about 1 1/2 hours. Remove pork from pan. Set aside. Strain liquid though fine-mesh sieve. Transfer 3 cups (750 mL) liquid to large pan (reserve remaining liquid for other cooking purposes; see Tip, page 64). Place pan over high heat and reduce by three-quarters. Set aside to cool.

Combine next 8 ingredients in medium bowl. Stir in liquid reduction. Fold in chopped nuts. Brush sauce generously over ribs. Bake in 400°F (200°C) oven for 10 minutes. Brush again with sauce and bake for an additional 10 minutes. Remove and let stand for 5 minutes before serving. Serves 5.

1 serving: 590 Calories; 15 g Total Fat (16 g Mono, 2 g Poly, 4 g Sat); 150 mg Cholesterol; 49 g Carbohydrate (2 g Fibre, 36 g Sugar); 64 g Protein; 1000 mg Sodium

blackberry ribs

Tangy and sweet, these ribs are equally good whether grilled on the barbecue or broiled.

Pork side ribs, cut into 2 rib sections	3 1/2 lbs.	1.6 kg
Blackberry jam (or jelly)	1/2 cup	125 mL
Ketchup	1/3 cup	75 mL
Steak sauce	1 tbsp.	15 mL
Dry mustard	1/2 tsp.	2 mL
Garlic powder	1/8 tsp.	0.5 mL

In a large saucepan, boil spareribs in enough water to cover for about 1 hour, until very tender. Drain. Arrange on greased baking sheet with sides. Line with greased foil for easy cleanup.

Mix remaining 5 ingredients in small saucepan. Heat, stirring often, until boiling. Simmer for 5 to 10 minutes. Brush hot ribs with glaze. Broil or barbecue for about 5 minutes per side. Serves 4.

1 serving: 910 Calories; 66 g Total Fat (0 g Mono, 0 g Poly, 21 g Sat); 230 mg Cholesterol; 32 g Carbohydrate (0 g Fibre, 29 g Sugar); 44 g Protein; 540 mg Sodium

five-spice ribs

Spicy, glazed ribs with a scrumptious flavour. Messy to eat—and that's half of the fun!

Pork side ribs, cut into 4 portions	4 lbs.	1.8 kg
Large onion, quartered	1	1
Bay leaves	2	2
Garlic cloves	6	6
Sherry (or alcohol-free sherry)	1 cup	250 mL
Indonesian sweet (or thick) soy sauce	1/4 cup	60 mL
Fancy (mild) molasses	3 tbsp.	45 mL
Lemon juice	2 tbsp.	30 mL
Celery seed	1 tsp.	5 mL
Paprika	1 tsp.	5 mL
Hot pepper sauce	1 tsp.	5 mL
Chinese five-spice powder	2 tsp.	10 mL

Put first 5 ingredients into stock pot or Dutch oven. Add enough water just to cover ribs. Bring to a boil. Reduce heat to medium-low. Simmer, covered, for 45 to 60 minutes until ribs are tender. Drain.

Combine remaining 7 ingredients in small bowl. Brush ribs with sauce. Preheat gas barbecue to medium-low. Place ribs on well-greased grill. Cook for about 5 minutes per side, basting with remaining sauce often, until glazed and browned. Serves 4.

1 serving: 980 Calories; 64 g Total Fat (28 g Mono, 6 g Poly, 24 g Sat); 245 mg Cholesterol; 30 g Carbohydrate (1 g Fibre, 21 g Sugar); 67 g Protein; 620 mg Sodium

glazed back ribs

A not-too-peppery glaze coats tender pork ribs. Add more jalapeño pepper and extra hot pepper sauce if you prefer a spicier bite.

Apple cider	2 cups	500 mL
Finely chopped red onion	1/3 cup	75 mL
Finely chopped jalapeño pepper (see Tip, page 64)	1 tbsp.	15 mL
Ketchup	1/3 cup	75 mL
Tomato paste (see Tip, page 64)	3 tbsp.	45 mL
Red wine vinegar	2 tbsp.	30 mL
Brown sugar, packed	2 tbsp.	30 mL
Hot pepper sauce	2 tbsp.	30 mL
Pepper	1/4 tsp.	1 mL
Pork back ribs (about 8 racks), cut into 4-bone portions	4 lbs.	1.8 kg

Combine first 3 ingredients in medium saucepan. Bring to a boil on medium-high. Reduce heat to medium. Boil gently, uncovered, for about 15 minutes until reduced to about 1 cup (250 mL) liquid.

Add next 6 ingredients. Stir. Remove from heat.

To preheat barbecue, turn on 1 burner. Adjust burner to maintain an interior barbecue temperature of medium-low. Place ribs, bone side down, on unlit side of greased grill. Brush with glaze. Close lid. Cook for 2 to 2 1/4 hours, turning ribs occasionally and brushing with glaze, until tender. Remove to large plate. Serves 8.

1 serving: 630 Calories; 47 g Total Fat (21 g Mono, 4 g Poly, 17 g Sat); 160 mg Cholesterol; 16 g Carbohydrate (trace Fibre, 15 g Sugar); 33 g Protein; 320 mg Sodium

tomatillo ribs

Tomatillos are believed to have originated in Mexico, and they are heavily featured in Mexican cuisine. Tomatillo salsa is usually labelled as salsa verde and can be found in the Mexican section of your local grocery store.

Chili powder	1 tbsp.	15 mL
Brown sugar, packed	2 tsp.	10 mL
Garlic powder	2 tsp.	10 mL
Onion powder	2 tsp.	10 mL
Smoked (sweet) paprika	1 tsp.	5 mL
Dried oregano	1 tsp.	5 mL
Salt	1 tsp.	5 mL
Pepper	1/2 tsp.	2 mL
Pork back ribs (about 2 racks)	3 lbs.	1.4 kg
Salsa verde (tomatillo salsa)	1 cup	250 mL

Combine first 8 ingredients in small bowl. Rub over ribs. Chill, covered, for 2 hours.

To preheat barbecue, turn on 1 burner. Adjust burner to maintain an interior barbecue temperature of medium. Place ribs, meat side down, on greased grill over unlit burner. Close lid. Cook for about 75 minutes, turning at halftime, until meat is tender and starts to pull away from bones.

Process salsa in blender until smooth. Brush over ribs. Close lid. Cook ribs for about 30 minutes, turning at halftime and brushing with salsa. Transfer to large serving plate. Cover with foil. Let stand for 10 minutes. Cut into 3-bone portions. Serves 8.

1 serving: 500 Calories; 40 g Total Fat (18 g Mono, 3.5 g Poly, 15 g Sat); 140 mg Cholesterol; 5 g Carbohydrate (trace Fibre; 2 g Sugar); 28 g Protein; 140 mg Sodium

curry coconut ribs

Creaminess, tangy freshness and chili heat combine with tender, fall-off-the-bone pork for a sumptuous update to traditional barbecued ribs.

Racks of pork side ribs (about 1 1/2 lbs., 680 g, each), trimmed of fat	2	2
Garlic cloves, sliced	5	5
Ginger root slices (1/4 inch, 6 mm, thick)	4	4
Seasoned salt	1 tbsp.	15 mL
Cooking oil	1/2 tsp.	2 mL
Red curry paste	1 tbsp.	15 mL
Can of coconut milk (14 oz., 398 mL)	1	1
Brown sugar, packed	3 tbsp.	45 mL
Soy sauce	3 tbsp.	45 mL
Lime juice	2 tbsp.	30 mL

Cut each rack of ribs in half. Combine next 3 ingredients and ribs in Dutch oven or large pot. Add water to cover and bring to a boil. Simmer, covered, on medium-low for about 1 hour until ribs are tender. Drain, discarding garlic and ginger. Transfer ribs to a 9 x 13 inch (23 x 33 cm) baking dish.

Heat cooking oil in saucepan on medium and add curry paste. Heat and stir for about 1 minute until curry is fragrant.

Add remaining 4 ingredients. Simmer, uncovered, for 10 minutes to blend flavours. Pour over ribs and turn to coat. Let stand for 30 minutes. Grill ribs on direct medium heat for about 15 minutes, turning often and brushing with curry mixture until ribs are glazed and heated through. Cut into 2-bone portions. Makes about 12 portions.

1 portion: 410 Calories; 34 g Total Fat (12 g Mono, 2.5 g Poly, 16 g Sat); 90 mg Cholesterol; 5 g Carbohydrate (0 g Fibre, 3 g Sugar); 21 g Protein; 370 mg Sodium

apple curry ribs

Apple and mild curry make for a perfect combination of flavours in these mouthwatering ribs. The spicy heat lingers but is mild overall, so the whole family will love them. Make sure there are plenty of napkins on hand!

Brown sugar, packed	1 tbsp.	15 mL
Garlic cloves, minced	2	2
(or 1/2 tsp., 2 mL, powder)		
Dried crushed chilies	1 tsp.	5 mL
Ground cumin	1 tsp.	5 mL
Ground ginger	1 tsp.	5 mL
Ground coriander	1/2 tsp	2 mL
Salt	1/2 tsp.	2 mL
Pepper	1/4 tsp.	1 mL
Pork back ribs (about 2 racks)	3 lbs.	1.4 kg
Sweetened applesauce	1 cup	250 mL
Hot curry paste	1 tbsp.	15 mL

Combine first 8 ingredients in small bowl. Rub mixture over ribs. Chill, covered, for 2 hours. To preheat barbecue, turn on 1 burner. Adjust burner to maintain an interior barbecue temperature of medium. Place ribs on greased grill over unlit burner. Close lid. Cook for about 1 1/4 hours, turning several times, until meat is tender and starts to pull away from bones.

Combine applesauce and curry paste in small bowl. Brush over ribs. Close lid. Cook ribs for about 30 minutes, turning several times and brushing with applesauce mixture, until meat is glazed. Transfer to large serving plate. Cover with foil. Let stand for 10 minutes. Cut into 3-bone portions. Makes about 9 portions.

1 portion: 460 Calories; 36 g Total Fat (16 g Mono, 3 g Poly, 13 g Sat); 120 mg Cholesterol; 8 g Carbohydrate (trace Fibre, 6 g Sugar); 25 g Protein; 270 mg Sodium

java ribs

The unique marinade, made with coffee, transforms tender pork ribs into a succulent feast!

Pork side ribs, cut into 3-bone portions	6 lbs.	2.7 kg
Bay leaves	2	2
Dried thyme	3/4 tsp.	4 mL
Onion salt	1/2 tsp.	2 mL
Pepper	1/2 tsp.	2 mL
Cold strong prepared coffee	1 1/4 cups	300 mL
Ketchup	1 1/4 cups	300 mL
Brown sugar, packed	2/3 cup	150 mL
Apple cider vinegar	1/2 cup	125 mL
Worcestershire sauce	4 tsp.	20 mL

Place ribs in large pot or Dutch oven. Add enough water to cover. Add next 4 ingredients. Bring to a boil on medium-high. Reduce heat to medium-low. Simmer, covered, for about 1 hour until pork is just tender. Drain and discard liquid. Set aside to cool.

Measure remaining 5 ingredients into large bowl. Stir until sugar is dissolved. Add ribs. Turn until coated. Let stand, covered, for 30 minutes. Drain, reserving marinade in medium saucepan. Bring reserved marinade to a boil on medium. Reduce heat to medium-low. Simmer, uncovered, for at least 5 minutes. Preheat barbecue to medium. Cook ribs on greased grill for 15 to 20 minutes, turning occasionally and brushing with reserved marinade, until glazed and heated through. Serves 8.

1 serving: 780 Calories; 56 g Total Fat (24 g Mono, 5 g Poly, 19 g Sat); 190 mg Cholesterol; 28 g Carbohydrate (0 g Fibre, 28 g Sugar); 37 g Protein; 710 mg Sodium

sticky ginger ribs

Two kinds of ginger, one from ginger ale, give these ribs subtle flavour. The kids will love these messy, tasty ribs for their sweet, tangy tomato sauce.

Ketchup	1 cup	250 mL
Lemon juice	3 tbsp.	45 mL
Brown sugar, packed	2 tbsp.	30 mL
Worcestershire sauce	1 tbsp.	15 mL
Dry mustard	2 tsp.	10 mL
Ground ginger	1 1/2 tsp.	7 mL
Garlic salt	1/2 tsp.	2 mL
Onion powder	1/2 tsp.	2 mL
Pepper	1/4 tsp.	1 mL
Sweet and sour cut pork ribs, trimmed of fat and cut into 6-bone portions	3 lbs.	1.4 kg
Cans of ginger ale (12 1/2 oz., 355 mL, each)	2	2

Combine first 9 ingredients in medium saucepan. Bring to a boil, stirring occasionally. Remove from heat.

Place ribs in large pot or Dutch oven. Pour ginger ale over top. Add water to cover. Bring to a boil. Reduce heat to medium. Simmer, uncovered, for about 1 hour until ribs are tender. Drain. Transfer to large bowl. Pour 3/4 cup (175 mL) ketchup mixture over top. Toss until coated. Preheat barbecue to medium. Place ribs on greased grill. Close lid. Cook for about 15 minutes, turning often and brushing with remaining ketchup mixture, until ribs are glazed and heated through. Cut into 3-bone portions. Makes 12 portions.

1 portion: 360 Calories; 27 g Total Fat (12 g Mono, 12.5 g Poly, 10 g Sat); 90 mg Cholesterol; 9 g Carbohydrate (0 g Fibre, 8 g Sugar) 19 g Protein; 430 mg Sodium

country-style pork ribs

Moist, tender pork with a golden glaze and a wonderful smoky taste that permeates the meat.

Barbecue sauce (mesquite or hickory flavour is best)	1 cup	250 mL
Liquid honey	1/4 cup	60 mL
Soy sauce	1 tbsp.	15 mL
Chopped onion	1/2 cup	125 mL
Garlic cloves, minced (or 1/2 tsp., 2 mL, powder), optional	2	2
Country-style pork rib ends	3 lbs.	1.4 kg
Mesquite (or hickory) wood chips	1 1/2 cups	375 mL

Combine first 5 ingredients in small bowl. Pour into shallow dish or resealable freezer bag. Add ribs. Turn to coat. Marinate, covered or sealed, in refrigerator for at least 4 hours or up to 24 hours, turning several times.

Put 1/2 of dry wood chips into smoker box. Soak remaining chips in water in medium bowl for 15 to 30 minutes. Drain. Place on top of dry chips. Close smoker box. Place on grill on 1 side of gas barbecue. Close lid. Heat barbecue to medium for 15 to 20 minutes until chips are smoking. Adjust burner under smoker box as necessary to keep it smoking. Adjust opposite burner to maintain medium-low barbecue temperature. Remove grill opposite smoker box using oven mitts. Place drip pan, with 1 inch (2.5 cm) water, directly on heat source. Replace grill. Drain and discard marinade. Arrange ribs on greased grill over drip pan. Close lid. Cook for 1 hour. Turn ribs. Replenish water in pan if necessary. Cook ribs for 15 to 20 minutes until tender and glazed. Serves 6.

1 serving: 460 Calories; 19 g Total Fat (8 g Mono, 2 g Poly, 6 g Sat); 160 mg Cholesterol; 36 g Carbohydrate (0 g Fibre, 11 g Sugar); 46 g Protein; 880 mg Sodium

dry curry ribs

Tender ribs smoked to perfection with a delicate curry flavour on the outside and moist meat on the inside.

Curry powder	2 tbsp.	30 mL
Cajun seasoning	2 tbsp.	30 mL
Brown sugar, packed	2 tbsp.	30 mL
Lemon pepper	2 tbsp.	30 mL
Dried oregano	1 tbsp.	15 mL
Garlic salt	2 tsp.	10 mL
Finely grated orange zest	1 tsp.	5 mL
Pork side ribs, cut into 4 portions	3 lbs.	1.4 kg
Maple wood chips	1 1/2 cups	375 mL

Combine first 7 ingredients in small bowl. Rub mixture over both sides of each portion of ribs. Place in shallow dish, on baking sheet or on platter. Marinate, covered, in refrigerator for at least 6 hours or overnight.

Put 1/2 of dry wood chips into smoker box. Soak remaining chips in water in medium bowl for 15 to 30 minutes. Drain. Place on top of dry chips. Close smoker box. Place on grill on 1 side of gas barbecue. Close lid. Heat barbecue to medium for 15 to 20 minutes until chips are smoking. Turn off burner opposite smoker box. Turn burner under smoker box to medium. Place ribs on greased grill on unlit side. Close lid. Cook for 1 to 1 1/2 hours, turning occasionally, until tender. Serves 4.

1 serving: 710 Calories; 51 g Total Fat (22 g Mono, 4.5 g Poly, 19 g Sat); 195 mg Cholesterol; 9 g Carbohydrate (1 g Fibre, 7 g Sugar); 53 g Protein; 1870 mg Sodium

plum ribs

These small ribs are coated in a sticky, sweet sauce that pairs perfectly with steamed jasmine rice. Garnish with green onion for a little flair.

Sweet and sour cut pork ribs, trimmed of fat and cut into 1-bone portions	3 1/2 lbs.	1.6 kg
Boiling water	4 cups	1 L
Water	1 cup	250 mL
Plum sauce	1/3 cup	75 mL
White vinegar	3 tbsp.	45 mL
Ketchup	3 tbsp.	45 mL
Soy sauce	2 tbsp.	30 mL
Brown sugar, packed	2 tbsp.	30 mL
Garlic cloves, minced (or 1/2 tsp., 2 mL, powder)	2	2
Chili sauce	2 tsp.	10 mL

Heat wok or medium saucepan on medium-high. Add ribs and boiling water. Bring to a boil. Boil, covered, for 30 minutes, stirring occasionally. Drain. Transfer ribs to bowl.

Add remaining 8 ingredients to hot wok. Stir until combined. Bring to a boil. Reduce heat to medium. Add ribs. Cook, uncovered, for about 20 minutes, stirring often, until sauce is thick and ribs are coated. Makes 8 cups (2 L).

1 cup (250 mL): 440 Calories: 33 g Total Fat (0 g Mono, 0 g Poly, 11 g Sat); 115 mg Cholesterol; 11 g Carbohydrate (0 g Fibre, 5 g Sugar); 23 g Protein; 510 mg Sodium

black bean pork ribs

Tender brown ribs in a rich, spicy sauce. Spoon the sauce over spaghetti squash for a delicious change!

Canola oil	1 tbsp.	15 mL
Sweet and sour cut pork ribs, trimmed of fat, cut into 1-bone portions	1 1/2 lbs.	680 g
Paprika	1 tsp.	5 mL
Salt	1/2 tsp.	2 mL
Pepper	1/8 tsp.	0.5 mL
Chili black bean sauce	2 tbsp.	30 mL
Brown sugar, packed	1 tbsp.	15 mL
Low-sodium soy sauce	1 tbsp.	15 mL
Rice vinegar	1 tbsp.	15 mL
Garlic cloves, minced (or 1/2 tsp., 2 mL, powder)	2	2
Finely grated, peeled ginger root	2 tsp.	10 mL
Water	1 1/2 cups	375 mL
Dry sherry	2 tbsp.	30 mL
Water	2 tbsp.	30 mL
Cornstarch	1 tbsp.	15 mL

Heat wok or large frying pan on medium-high. Add canola oil. Add next 4 ingredients. Stir-fry for about 5 minutes until ribs are browned. Remove ribs with slotted spoon to large plate.

Reduce heat to medium. Add next 6 ingredients. Heat and stir for 1 to 2 minutes until brown sugar is dissolved.

Add first amount of water and sherry. Stir. Bring to a boil. Add ribs. Reduce heat to medium-low. Simmer, covered, for 45 to 60 minutes until pork is tender.

Stir second amount of water into cornstarch in small cup until smooth. Add to pork mixture. Heat and stir for about 3 minutes until sauce is boiling and slightly thickened. Serves 4.

1 serving: 380 Calories; 27 g Total Fat (12 g Mono, 3.5 g Poly, 9 g Sat); 88 mg Cholesterol; 8 g Carbohydrate (trace Fibre, 4 g Sugar); 25 g Protein; 600 mg Sodium

easiest ribs

This is an effortless slow cooker recipe that yields fantastic results.
For best results, use well-trimmed ribs.

Fancy (mild) molasses	1/3 cup	75 mL
Low-sodium soy sauce	1/3 cup	75 mL
Garlic cloves, minced (or 3/4 tsp., 4 mL, powder)	3	3
Dried crushed chilies	1/4 tsp.	1 mL
Sweet and sour cut pork ribs, trimmed of fat and cut into 1-bone portions	3 1/2 lbs	1.6 kg

Combine first 4 ingredients in 3 1/2 quart (3.5 L) slow cooker.

Add ribs. Stir until coated. Cook on Low for 7 to 8 hours or on High for 3 1/2 to 4 hours, stirring once or twice, until very tender. Serves 6.

1 serving: 680 Calories; 46 g Total Fat (20 g Mono, 4 g Poly, 17 g Sat); 175 mg Cholesterol; 16 g Carbohydrate (0 g Fibre, 12 g Sugar); 48 g Protein; 750 mg Sodium

teriyaki-glazed ribs

Pair these sweet, saucy ribs with a side of grilled or stir-fried veggies and jasmine or basmati rice.

Water	8 cups	2 L
Pork back ribs	4 lbs.	1.8 kg
Teriyaki sauce	1/2 cup	125 mL
Liquid honey	1/2 cup	125 mL
Dijon mustard	1/3 cup	75 mL
Worcestershire sauce	1/4 cup	60 mL
Hot pepper sauce	1 tbsp.	15 mL
Garlic cloves, minced	5	5

Fill large pot or Dutch oven with water and bring to a boil. Add ribs. Turn heat down and let simmer for 20 minutes. Remove ribs to shallow dish.

Combine remaining 6 ingredients in small pot. Simmer, uncovered, for about 10 minutes until sauce is reduced to a glaze-like consistency. Preheat barbecue to medium. Brush ribs with sauce and place, meat side down, on greased grill. Flip every 5 minutes, brushing with sauce, for a total of 20 minutes. Remove from barbecue and cut into 3-bone portions. Serves 4.

1 serving: 1480 Calories; 107 g Total Fat (48 g Mono, 9 g Poly, 40 g Sat); 365 mg Cholesterol; 52 g Carbohydrate (0 g Fibre, 45 g Sugar); 74 g Protein; 1410 mg Sodium

baked stuffed ribs

Think stuffing is only for turkey? Think again! Nestled between two layers of ribs, the dressing cooks to perfection. Pair this dish with your favourite veggies to round out the meal.

Pork side ribs	6 lbs.	2.7 kg
Butter (or margarine)	3 tbsp.	45 mL
Chopped onion	2 cups	500 mL
Egg	1	1
Dry bread crumbs	3 cups	750 mL
Poultry seasoning	1 tsp.	5 mL
Celery salt	1/2 tsp.	2 mL
Salt	1 tsp.	5 mL
Pepper	1/4 tsp.	1 mL
Milk, enough to moisten, if needed		

Lay half of ribs in strip in roaster.

Melt butter in frying pan. Add onion and cook until clear and soft.

Beat egg in medium bowl. Add next 5 ingredients. Add onion. Stir. If dry, add a little milk to moisten. Spoon over ribs. Cover with remaining strip of ribs. Bake, covered, in 350°F (180°C) oven until tender, about 2 1/2 hours. Serves 8.

1 serving: 890 Calories; 66 g Total Fat (28 g Mono, 6 g Poly, 26 g Sat); 275 mg Cholesterol; 4 g Carbohydrate (trace Fibre, 2 g Sugar); 65 g Protein; 510 mg Sodium

apricot tequila ribs

Sticky and delicious. A fiesta in your mouth!

Racks of beef back ribs, bone-in, trimmed of fat and cut into 1-bone portions	4 lbs.	1.8 kg
Sliced onion	1/2 cup	125 mL
Cumin seed	1 tsp.	5 mL
Bay leaves	2	2
Apricot jam	1/2 cup	125 mL
Tomato paste (see Tip, page 64)	3 tbsp.	45 mL
Tequila	2 tbsp.	30 mL
Garlic clove, minced (or 1/4 tsp., 1 mL, powder)	1	1
Salt	1/2 tsp.	2 mL
Dried crushed chilies	1/2 tsp.	2 mL
Grated lime zest	1/2 tsp.	2 mL

Place first 4 ingredients in large pot or Dutch oven. Add water to cover. Bring to a boil. Reduce heat to medium-low. Simmer, covered, for about 90 minutes until ribs are tender. Drain. Discard onion, cumin seed and bay leaves.

Combine remaining 7 ingredients in small bowl. Brush over ribs. Arrange, meat side down, on foil-lined baking sheet with sides. Bake in 450°F (230°C) oven for 10 minutes. Turn over. Brush with remaining jam mixture. Bake for about 10 minutes until meat is tender, glazed and pulling away from bones. Cover with foil. Let stand for 10 minutes. Serves 4.

1 serving: 400 Calories; 25 g Total Fat (11 g Mono, 1 g Poly, 10 g Sat); 60 mg Cholesterol; 30 g Carbohydrate (trace Fibre, 28 g Sugar); 15 g Protein; 630 mg Sodium

short ribs

Tender beef with a sweet and savory sauce. Serve with white rice and steamed vegetables.

Boneless beef short ribs, cut into serving-size pieces	2 lbs.	900 g
Chili sauce	1/2 cup	125 mL
Grape jelly	1/3 cup	75 mL
Medium onion, chopped	1	1
Brown sugar, packed	1 tbsp.	15 mL
Prepared mustard	1 tbsp.	15 mL
Dried rosemary, crushed	1/2 tsp.	2 mL
Lemon juice	1 tbsp.	15 mL
Salt	1 tsp.	5 mL
Pepper	1/2 tsp.	2 mL

Arrange ribs in small roasting pan.

Combine remaining 9 ingredients in small bowl. Spoon over ribs. Bake, covered, in 300°F (150°C) oven for about 4 hours until tender. Remove ribs to serving plate. Skim off fat in pan and discard. Pour remaining sauce over ribs. Serves 5.

1 serving: 430 Calories; 19 g Total Fat (8 g Mono, 0.5 g Poly, 8 g Sat); 85 mg Cholesterol; 28 g Carbohydrate (trace Fibre, 18 g Sugar); 36 g Protein; 1020 mg Sodium

short rib dinner

The vegetables and meat cook in the same roasting pan for a homey dish with little fuss or cleanup. The ultimate comfort food.

Beef short ribs, cut up	3 1/2 lbs.	1.6 kg
White vinegar	3 tbsp.	45 mL
Brown sugar, packed	3 tbsp.	45 mL
Salt	1 1/2 tsp.	7 mL
Pepper	1/2 tsp.	2 mL
Beef bouillon powder	2 tsp.	10 mL
Garlic powder	1/4 tsp.	1 mL
Prepared horseradish	1 tbsp.	15 mL
Sliced onion	1 cup	250 mL
Medium potatoes, quartered	4	4
Peeled baby carrots	24	24
All-purpose flour	1/4 cup	60 mL
Salt	1/2 tsp.	2 mL

Place ribs on rack in broiling tray. Broil each side for 5 minutes until browned. Place in small roaster.

Mix next 7 ingredients in small bowl. Pour over short ribs.

Add enough water to barely cover beef. Bake, covered, in 325ºF (160ºC) oven for 1 1/2 to 2 hours until almost tender.

Add onion, potato and carrots. Bake, covered, for 1 hour until beef is very tender and vegetables are cooked. Strain liquid into measuring cup. Add water to make 2 cups (500 mL).

Gradually whisk strained liquid into flour and salt in small saucepan until smooth. Heat and stir until boiling and thickened. Makes 2 cups (500 mL). Serve with ribs and vegetables. Serves 4.

1 serving: 760 Calories; 33 g Total Fat (14 g Mono, 0 g Poly, 14 g Sat); 155 mg Cholesterol; 62 g Carbohydrate (5 g Fibre, 16 g Sugar); 57 g Protein; 1720 mg Sodium

saucy braised beef ribs

Braising may be a little time consuming but results in tender, flavourful ribs. They're well worth the wait! Serve the delicious sauce over polenta or pasta for a complete meal.

Racks of beef back ribs, bone-in (2 lbs., 900 g, each), trimmed of fat and cut into 1-bone portions	2	2
Pepper	1/2 tsp.	2 mL
Sliced onion	2 cups	500 mL
Sliced carrot	1 cup	250 mL
Bay leaves	2	2
Prepared beef broth	2 cups	500 mL
Dry (or alcohol-free) red wine	1 cup	250 mL
All-purpose flour	2 tbsp.	30 mL
Dijon mustard	2 tbsp.	30 mL
Italian seasoning	1/2 tsp.	2 mL
Balsamic vinegar	1/2 tsp.	2 mL

Arrange ribs, meat side up, in large roasting pan. Sprinkle with pepper. Cook, uncovered, in 450°F (230°C) oven for about 40 minutes until ribs are browned. Drain and discard fat from pan. Reduce heat to 350°F (175°C).

Scatter next 3 ingredients around ribs.

Whisk next 5 ingredients in medium bowl until smooth. Pour over ribs and vegetables. Stir. Cook, covered, for about 2 hours, turning ribs at halftime, until meat is tender and starts to pull away from bones. Transfer ribs to serving platter. Cover to keep warm.

Remove and discard bay leaves from onion mixture. Skim and discard fat from cooking liquid. Transfer to blender or food processor. Add vinegar. Carefully process until smooth, following manufacturer's instructions for processing hot liquids. Makes about 2 cups (500 mL) sauce. Serve with ribs. Serves 6.

1 serving: 610 Calories; 31 g Total Fat (13 g Mono, 1 g Poly, 13 g Sat); 145 mg Cholesterol; 11 g Carbohydrate (1 g Fibre, 3 g Sugar); 61 g Protein; 580 mg Sodium

kalbi

Korean barbecue is justifiably famous. The sweet, gingery kiwi marinade imbues these short ribs with delicious flavour and remarkable tenderness. Be careful not to marinate for too long as the texture of the meat will break down. Garnish this dish with sliced green onion and toasted sesame seeds.

Brown sugar, packed	1/2 cup	125 mL
Mirin	1/2 cup	125 mL
Soy sauce	1/2 cup	125 mL
Kiwifruit	1	1
Rice vinegar	1/4 cup	60 mL
Finely grated ginger root	2 tbsp.	30 mL
Garlic cloves, minced	6	6
Sesame oil	2 tbsp.	30 mL
Pepper	1 tsp.	5 mL
Korean-style beef short ribs	3 lbs.	1.4 kg

Process first 9 ingredients in a blender or food processor until smooth. Reserve 1/2 cup (125 mL) marinade and chill.

Pour remaining marinade into a large resealable freezer bag. Add ribs and marinate in refrigerator for 4 hours. Drain and discard marinade. Cook ribs on greased grill on medium-high, brushing with reserved marinade, for 4 minutes per side until well done. Serves 4.

1 serving: 1460 Calories; 110 g Total Fat (47 g Mono, 7 g Poly, 43 g Sat); 250 mg Cholesterol; 54 g Carbohydrate; Trace Fibre; Sugar 49 g; 61 g Protein; 2070 mg Sodium

chipotle-braised short ribs

Short ribs are meaty, beefy ribs. They need a long, slow cooking time, and they're not typically cooked on the grill. In this recipe, the ribs are dusted with a dry rub and then slow-cooked over indirect heat for 3 to 4 hours, until the meat falls off the bone. Because these short ribs are so rich, you don't need many to make a great meal.

Dried oregano	3 tbsp.	45 mL
Dried parsley flakes	2 tsp.	10 mL
Dried thyme leaves	2 tbsp.	30 mL
Kosher salt	2 tbsp.	30 mL
Cracked black pepper	1 tbsp.	15 mL
Ground chipotle powder	2 tsp	10 mL
Garlic powder	1 tsp	5 mL
Brown sugar	1 tbsp.	15 mL
Beef short ribs, trimmed of almost all fat	3 lbs.	1.4 kg
Barbecue sauce	1/2 cup	125 mL
Beer	1/2 cup	125 mL

Preheat one side of barbecue to low and leave the other side off. Mix first 8 ingredients in small bowl or place in plastic bag.

In small batches, dredge short ribs in rub and place on off side of barbecue. Close lid and cook for 3 hours, checking about every 45 minutes, flipping meat and brushing it with beer mixture. When ribs are done—when meat is falling off bones—brush again with beer mixture. Remove from heat and serve. Serves 6.

1 serving: 350 Calories; 19 g Total Fat (8 g Mono, 0 g Poly, 8 g Sat); 90 mg Cholesterol; 13 g Carbohydrate (1 g Fibre, 2 g Sugar); 30 g Protein; 1550 mg Sodium

savoury short ribs

A simple marinade elevates a tougher cut of meat into something spectacular!

Can of tomato sauce (7 1/2 oz., 213 mL)	1	1
Apple cider vinegar	1/2 cup	125 mL
Cooking oil	1/4 cup	60 mL
Granulated sugar	1 1/2 tbsp.	22 mL
Dry onion flakes	1 tbsp.	15 mL
Worcestershire sauce	2 tsp.	10 mL
Prepared mustard	1 tsp.	5 mL
Chili powder	1 tsp.	5 mL
Pepper	1/2 tsp.	2 mL
Garlic powder	1/4 tsp.	1 mL
Beef short ribs, bone-in	3 lbs.	1.4 kg

Combine first 10 ingredients in small bowl.

Place short ribs in shallow baking dish. Pour marinade over ribs. Turn until coated. Cover with plastic wrap. Marinate in refrigerator for at least 6 hours or overnight, turning occasionally. Drain, reserving marinade in small saucepan. Bring reserved marinade to a boil on medium. Reduce heat to medium-low. Simmer, uncovered, for at least 5 minutes. Let ribs stand until room temperature before cooking. Preheat barbecue to low. Place ribs on greased grill. Close lid. Cook for about 45 minutes, turning occasionally and brushing with reserved marinade, until tender. Serves 4.

1 serving: 590 Calories; 42 g Total Fat (20 g Mono, 3.5 g Poly, 13 g Sat); 130 mg Cholesterol; 11 g Carbohydrate (1 g Fibre, 8 g Sugar); 45 g Protein; 610 mg Sodium

chili cherry beef ribs

Sweet cherry blends with chili warmth for a full-bodied sauce that will have your dining companions begging for your secret.

Cherry jam	1 cup	250 mL
Hickory barbecue sauce	1/3 cup	75 mL
Chili paste (sambal oelek)	1 tbsp.	15 mL
Racks of beef back ribs (2 lbs., 900 g, each), trimmed of fat	2	2
Seasoned salt	1 tbsp.	15 mL

Combine first 3 ingredients in a saucepan. Gently boil on medium for 5 minutes to blend flavours.

Rub ribs with seasoned salt. Place drip pan on 1 burner. To preheat barbecue, turn on burner opposite drip pan. Adjust burner to maintain interior barbecue temperature of medium. Place ribs, meat side down, on greased grill over drip pan. Cook for 1 hour. Turn and cook for about 1 hour, brushing occasionally with cherry mixture, until meat is tender, glazed and pulling away from bones. Cover with foil and let stand for 10 minutes. Cut into 1-bone portions. Makes about 14 ribs.

1 rib: 500 Calories; 38 g Total Fat (16 g Mono, 1.5 g Poly, 16 g Sat); 95 mg Cholesterol; 17 g Carbohydrate (0 g Fibre, 14 g Sugar); 21 g Protein; 500 mg Sodium

satay beef ribs

These finger-lickin', tender ribs get their rich flavour from a delicious, aromatic peanut and chili-infused sauce.

Thai peanut sauce	1 cup	250 mL
Canned coconut milk	1/2 cup	125 mL
Finely chopped Thai hot chili peppers (see Tip, page 64), or 1/2 tsp. (2 mL) cayenne pepper	2 tsp.	10 mL
Racks of beef back ribs, bone-in (2 lbs., 900 g, each), trimmed of fat	2	2
Salt	2 tsp.	10 mL

Combine first 3 ingredients in small bowl.

Sprinkle both sides of ribs with salt. Place drip pan on 1 burner. To preheat barbecue, turn on burner opposite drip pan. Adjust burner to maintain interior barbecue temperature of medium. Place ribs, meat side down, on greased grill over drip pan. Close lid. Cook for 1 hour. Turn ribs. Cook for about 1 hour, brushing occasionally with peanut sauce mixture, until meat is tender, glazed and pulling away from bones. Transfer to cutting board. Cover with foil. Let stand for 10 minutes. Cut into 1-bone portions. Makes about 14 ribs.

1 rib: 440 Calories; 36 g Total Fat (14 g Mono, 1 g Poly, 15 g Sat); 90 mg Cholesterol; 5 g Carbohydrate (trace Fibre, 3 g Sugar); 23 g Protein; 810 mg Sodium

recipe index

topical tips

Handling hot peppers: Hot peppers contain capsaicin in the seeds and ribs. Removing the seeds and ribs will reduce the heat. Wear rubber gloves when handling hot peppers and avoid touching your eyes. Wash your hands well afterward.

How to make tamarind liquid: For 1/2 cup (250 mL) of tamarind liquid, add 1/4 cup (60 mL) tamarind pulp to small bowl. Pour 3/4 cup (175 mL) boiling water over pulp, stirring to break up pulp. Let stand for 5 minutes. Press through a fine-meshed sieve and discard solids.

Leftover roasting liquid: The liquid reserved from roasting ribs can be used for a number of purposes including soup, sauces or even to spruce up your next pasta dish. It will keep in the fridge for up to 4 days or in the freezer for up to 6 months.

Tomato paste: If a recipe calls for less than an entire can of tomato paste, freeze the unopened can for 30 minutes. Open both ends and push the contents through one end. Slice off only what you need. Freeze the remaining paste in a resealable freezer bag or plastic wrap for future use.

Nutrition Information Guidelines

Each recipe is analyzed using the Canadian Nutrient File from Health Canada, which is based on the United States Department of Agriculture (USDA) Nutrient Database.

- If more than one ingredient is listed (such as "butter or hard margarine"), or if a range is given (1 – 2 tsp., 5 – 10 mL), only the first ingredient or first amount is analyzed.

- For meat, poultry and fish, the serving size per person is based on the recommended 4 oz. (113 g) uncooked weight (without bone), which is 2 – 3 oz. (57 – 85 g) cooked weight (without bone)— approximately the size of a deck of playing cards.

- Milk used is 1% M.F. (milk fat), unless otherwise stated.

- Cooking oil used is canola oil, unless otherwise stated.

- Ingredients indicating "sprinkle," "optional" or "for garnish" are not included in the nutrition information.

- The fat in recipes and combination foods can vary greatly depending on the sources and types of fats used in each specific ingredient. For these reasons, the count of saturated, monounsaturated and polyunsaturated fats may not add up to the total fat content.